Pachelbel's Canon

Johann Pachelbel
Arr. by Wesley Schaum

Andante espressivo ♩= 84-92

17
mp
f
21
f
mp
25
29
mf
ff
rit.

Stars and Stripes Forever

John Philip Sousa
Arr. by Wesley Schaum

Allegro ♩= 118-126

* The dotted 8th + 16th rhythm may be taught by rote.

Take Me Out to the Ball Game

Music by Albert von Tilzer
Words by Jack Norworth
Arr. by John W. Schaum

Vivace ♩ = 160-180

17
root, root, root for the home team, If
21
they don't win it's a shame. For it's
f
25
one, two, three strikes, you're out at the
29
old ball game.

Für Elise

Ludwig van Beethoven
Arr. by Wesley Schaum

Moderato ♩= 112-126

16
20
dim.
p
24
28
mp
8vb

ISBN-13: 978-1-4950-8081-4
Distributed By
HAL LEONARD
00645111 9 781495 080814

EXCLUSIVELY
DISTRIBUTED BY
HAL LEONARD
00645111
U.S. $4.95
0 08148 01702 7
1702